P9-EGJ-683

LETTERS AND LEADERSHIP

By the same author:

America's Coming-of-Age

The World of H. G. Wells

The Malady of the Ideal
   Essays on Amiel, etc.

The Wine of the Puritans:
   A Study of Present-Day America

John Addington Symonds:
   A Biographical Study

LETTERS AND LEADERSHIP

BY

VAN WYCK BROOKS

NEW YORK

B. W. HUEBSCH

MCMXVIII

COPYRIGHT, 1918, BY
B. W. HUEBSCH

PRINTED IN U. S. A.

It is curious to me that while so many voices, pens, minds, in the press, lecture-rooms, in our Congress, etc., are discussing intellectual topics, pecuniary dangers, legislative problems, the suffrage, tariff and labor questions, and the various business and benevolent needs of America, with propositions, remedies, often worth deep attention, there is one need, a hiatus the profoundest, that no eye seems to perceive, no voice to state. Our fundamental want to-day in the United States, with closest, amplest reference to present conditions, and to the future, is of a class, and the clear idea of a class, of native authors, literatuses, . . . permeating the whole mass of American mentality, taste, belief, breathing into it a new breath of life, giving it decision, affecting politics far more than the popular superficial suffrage, with results inside and underneath the elections of Presidents or Congresses —radiating, begetting appropriate teachers schools, manners, and as its grandest result accomplishing . . . a religious and moral character beneath the political and productive and intellectual bases of the States. . . . View'd to-day, from a point of view sufficiently over-arching, the problem of humanity all over the civilized world is social and religious, and is to be finally met and treated by literature.

—WHITMAN, *Democratic Vistas.*

PREFACE

M. Pierre de Lanux's *Young France and New America* will for the first time bring to the attention of a large class in this country a certain question over which our own writers have long been meditating, without being able to arrive at very definite conclusions.

M. de Lanux is the ambassador of a group of ideas and tendencies, in their infancy before the war, and still at the awkward age where they have to be loved a little before they can be understood at all. He has in mind, if I am not mistaken, a sort of conquest of the world carried out by the common action of the young people of all nations. Conquest, I say; I mean rather the sloughing of the old skin of society, the conscious and deliberate formulation of a new way of living, a new way of seeing life and arranging its conditions. Let us say that industrialism has developed among the nations a certain community of experience, and that this community of experience has in turn given birth to certain universal desires, emotions, hopes, ideas, and plans, universal, yes, even because of the war. Well, M. de Lanux constantly touches upon this group of desires, emotions, hopes, ideas, and plans. The writers from whom he quotes, the leaders of the young French intellectual class during the twentieth century, have ardently expressed perhaps the greater part of them. Is it necessary to mention Verhaeren, for example, a "good European" if there ever was one, the spokesman of modern humanity? And behind Verhaeren there is Whitman, whose influence on the French literature of to-day, M. de Lanux says, may well be called decisive. What do they portend, these writers, if it is not a heightened common consciousness in all who are still young enough in spirit to harbor generous hopes for civilization, a common aim leading them to struggle for a world that is able to keep and use the whole of its creative energy?

I do not mean that M. de Lanux develops this general thesis. But it is, I believe, the matrix of his argument. And it implies that if we are to develop this common aim, if we are to unite in this common programme, it is of the highest importance for us to understand the unique conditions that hamper the creative life in each individual country. What we want is the fullest and the freest expression of every people along the lines of its own genius, for it is of the nature of the creative spirit that its manifestations cannot conflict with one another and that the more various they are the richer and the more harmonious life becomes. That is why M. de Lanux, in selecting certain of our writers to translate into French, says that the more genuinely American they are the more France will be inclined to welcome them.

Now, there is something so disinterested and so beneficent in the French spirit and we feel so keenly our debt to it at the present time that we are much more disposed to be virtuous for France's sake than for the beautiful eyes of virtue itself. If, then, M. de Lanux tells us that his countrymen are certain to rejoice in the work of Vachel Lindsay, whose "muse essentially belongs to Springfield, Illinois, and knows no other shores," adding that "that is precisely why we shall be glad to welcome her," is it not the simplest of all deductions that we ought to set to work immediately producing as many poets as the homely muse of America can be induced to yield? I say this lightly because I want to take advantage of the present French alliance that apparently appeals so strongly to the common sense of the average American of the dominant class. In point of fact, of course, it implies a complete reorientation of American life. This of itself the average American of the dominant class could never be brought to contemplate. But how far would he not be reconciled to it if he were obliged to see that it is merely the logical outcome of his own loyalties in the war and that the more closely he draws to any of the societies of Europe the more he will have to surrender the baser elements of his own Americanism?

We speak of the obligations the war has laid upon us. Have we in fact begun to realize how grave they are? We say that the time has come for us to play our part among the societies of the world. But has it occurred to us that this means infinitely more than "men, money, and ships," that it requires nothing less than a mobilization of new, characteristic, and unique forces for the universal contest between darkness and light? Let us say that, thanks largely to our isolation, the spirit of our life in the past has been innocent of many of those baser elements in European life that produced the war. Let us say this, if we find it comforting, for it is true. But what have we to put beside those finer elements in European life that the war has not been able to destroy and that are even

now giving birth to whatever the ruture seems
to hold of promise for the human spirit? A
great deal, I should say, but little indeed in
presentable form. That is what enables our
unkinder critics to assert, with a certain air of
plausibility, that we really have nothing at all.

Frankly, with full recognition of the facts
of historic necessity, what is the present aspect
of our American life? We have been a primitive people, faced with an all but impossible
task. But is it not abundantly evident now
that we have accomplished this task and that
most of the customs we developed in the process
of meeting it have long since passed into the
limbo of "good customs that corrupt the
world"? The struggle that has hitherto en-
gaged us has been a struggle not between the
more creative and the less creative in man, but
between man and nature, and the impulse that
has determined it has come not from the pres-
sure of humane desires within, but from the
existence, the allure, and the eventual decay of

material opportunities outside. How shall one characterize the social result of that contest, that necessary contest, fraught with so much bitterness which we have cloaked in optimism in order to be able to endure it at all? The fierce, rudimentary mass-mind of America, like that of some inchoate primeval monster, relentlessly concentrated in the appetite of the moment, knows nothing of its own vast, inert, nerveless body, encrusted with parasites. One looks out to-day over the immense vista of our society, stretching westward in a succession of dreary steppes, and one realizes what it means to possess no cultural tradition filling in the interstices of energy and maintaining a steady current of life over and above the ebb and flow of individual purposes, of individual destinies! Our life is like a badly motivated novel, full of genius but written with an eye to quick returns, a novel that possesses no leading theme and alternates in style between journalese and purple patches, while every character goes its own arbitrary way, failing of its full effect. We are a population at sixes and sevens, holding among all classes and at all levels of development scarcely any common conviction save one, that "the essential preoccupation of youth," as one of our admired novelists put it the other day, is "organizing a living."

Such is the present aspect of our society and, like children whistling in the dark, we reassure one another that we like it and find it good. How simple we are! How little we know of the realities that our unconscious life reveals to the least experienced observer! Have we never tried to explain to ourselves that weary, baffled expression one sees in so many thousand middle-aged American faces, typical American faces, "successful" faces, the faces of bewildered men like Mr. Henry Ford? Has it never occurred to us to compare Mr. Ford's face with Mr. Ford's recent career? Has it never occurred to us that Mr. Ford is merely one of an immense class of men who have discovered that business somehow fails to fulfill their spiritual needs and have reached out from it only to find themselves lost in a maze of wider relationships with which no technique that they possess enables them to cope?

I think, indeed, that we could hardly find a more perfect symbol of American life in the present decade than Mr. Ford presents—Mr. Ford and his millions and his peace ship, and the total failure of these elements to coalesce in any effective purpose. If, therefore, we are dreaming of a "national culture," it is because our characteristic idealism has itself forced the issue. The gifts we possess are unique gifts, but of what avail are these gifts if we have no technique that enables them to find their mark? And what sort of technique will ever do this that has not arisen out of a consciousness of those gifts, that is not peculiar as they are peculiar and so adapted as to make them yield their fullest value? We wish to play our part in the higher life of the world, and we are incapable of doing so because we have no organized higher life of our own. Could there be a more unmistakable demand for just that release, that synthesis of the creative energies of the younger generation which M. de Lanux proposes and which the younger generation itself desires more deeply even than it knows?

It is in the hope of partially preparing the way for that synthesis that the following pages have been written. "We have striven, perhaps in vain," wrote Professor Barrett Wendell once, "to maintain a country where men shall be free to win not their aspirations, but their deserts." But aspirations *are* deserts in a great society, a society as great as America now for the first time has the opportunity to be. How can it seize that opportunity? Only, as I have said, by fully understanding the conditions that hamper its creative life. The reader will find these pages largely historical and all too largely negative. I hope, however, that he will find also between the lines certain suggestions of a programme for the future.

CONTENTS

LETTERS AND LEADERSHIP

CHAPTER I

OLD AMERICA

I

THERE is a certain spot in New York where I often ruminate in the summer noontime, a lonely, sunny, windy plaza surrounded by ramshackle hoardings and warehouses unfinished and already half in ruin. It is the fag end of a great cross-town thoroughfare, a far-thrown tentacle, as it were, of the immense monster one hears roaring not so far away, a tentacle that lies there sluggish and prone in the dust, overtaken by a sort of palsy. To the right and left stretches one of those interminable sunswept avenues that flank the city on east and west, wide, silent, and forsaken, perpetually vibrating in the blue haze that ascends from its hot cobblestones, bordered on one side by rickety wharves, on the other by a succession of tumble-down tenements left there like the sea-wrack at the ebb of the tide. For scarcely a living thing lingers here about the frayed edges of the town; it is as if one had been suddenly set down in the outskirts of some pioneer city on the plains of the Southwest, one of those half-built cities that sprawl out over the prairie, their long streets hectically alive in the center but gradually shedding their population and the few poor trees that mitigate the sun's glare, till at last, all but obliterated in alkali dust, they lose themselves in the sand and the silence.

All our towns and cities, I think, have this family likeness and share this alternating aspect of life and death—New York as much as the merest concoction of corrugated iron and clapboards thrown together beside a Western railway to fulfill some fierce evanescent impulse of pioneering enterprise. Like a field given over to fireworks, they have their points of light and heat, a district, a street, a group of streets where excitement gathers and life is tense and everything spins and whirls; and round about lie heaps of ashes, burned-out frames, seared enclosures, abandoned machinery, and all the tokens of a prodigal and long-spent energy.

But it is the American village that most betrays the impulse of our civilization, a civilization that perpetually overreaches itself only to be obliged to surrender again and again to nature everything it has gained. How many thousand villages, frost-bitten, palsied, full of a morbid, bloodless death-in-life, villages that have lost, if they ever possessed, the secret of self-perpetuation, lie scattered across the continent! Even in California I used to find them on long cross-country walks, villages often enough not half a century old but in a state of essential decay. Communities that have come into being on the flood-tide of an enterprise too rapidly worked out, they all signify some lost cause of a material kind that has left humanity high and dry; like the neutral areas in an old painting where the color, incompetently mixed and of perishable quality, has evaporated with time.

I suppose it is only natural in the West, these decayed settlements where time has taken so seriously, as it were, mankind's deliberate challenge to permanence. What shocks one is to realize that our Eastern villages, the seats of all the civilization we have, are themselves scarcely anything but the waste and ashes of pioneering, and that no inner fire has taken possession of the hearth where that original flame so long since burned itself out.

Off and on during the summers I have stayed in one of those ancient Long Island villages that still seem to preserve a little of the atmosphere of the early Republic. The crazy, weather-beaten houses that hold themselves up among their unkempt acres with a kind of angular dignity, the rotting porches and the stench of decay that hangs about their walls, the weed-choked gardens, the insect-ridden fruit trees, the rusty litter along the roads, the gaunt, silent farmers that stalk by in the dusk—how over-whelmingly they seem to betray a losing fight against the wilderness! For generations every man has gone his own way and sought his own luck. Nature has been robbed and despoiled and wasted for the sake of private and tempo-rary gains, and now, having no more easy re-wards to offer, it is taking its revenge on a race that has been too impatient and self-seeking to master its inner secrets. Incapable of co-oper-ating with nature, of lying fallow, of merging themselves, as it were, in the great current of life, they have accumulated no buoyant fund of instinct and experience, and each generation, a little more spiritually impoverished than the last, runs out the ever-shortening tether of self-reliance. Still pioneers, pioneers or nothing, they have lost the sap of adventure without developing beyond the stage of improvisation.

It is all so familiar, so intensely American, and yet the warm ancestral bond eludes one so! One looks out over a landscape everywhere abundant and propitious, but still in some way, after so many years of tillage, unimpregnated by human destiny, almost wholly wanting in that subtle fusion of natural and human elements which everywhere the European landscape suggests. For Europe is alive in all its members; in its loneliest and most isolated corner there is hardly a hamlet where life does not still persist, as green and warm and ruddy as the heart of an old olive tree. Some profound inertia, some imperturbable tenacity of the spirit, has prevented it from quite surrendering to nature anything, a bit of ground, a house, a road, that has once passed into the keeping of the race. And thus it is that while the conquest has been slow and laborious, invention tardy, ideas few, means inadequate, something cumulative survives.

Old American things are old as nothing else anywhere in the world is old, old without majesty, old without mellowness, old without pathos, just shabby and bloodless and worn out. That is the feeling that comes over one in villages like this, capable only of being galvanized by some fresh current of enterprise into a semblance of animation. Inhabited as they have always been by a race that has never cultivated life for its own sake, a race that has lived and built and worked always conscious of the possibility of a greater advantage to be found elsewhere, there is no principle of life working in them, three hundred years of effort having bred none of the indwelling spirit of continuity.

II

"Why is it," asks the author of *Jude the Obscure*, "that these preternaturally old boys always come out of new countries?" It was the spectacle of Jude himself, transplanted from Australia into the midst of the ancient peasantry of southern England, that prompted the question, and I remember with what force it came into my mind once, during a brief visit in Oxford, when, accustomed as my eyes for the moment were to the jocund aspect of young England in flannels, I came upon a company of Rhodes scholars from across the Atlantic. Pallid and wizened, little old men they seemed, rather stale and flat and dry; and I said to myself, it is a barren soil these men have sprung from,—plainly they have never known a day of good growing weather.

They might not have been typical Rhodes scholars, these men—I don't pretend to any wide knowledge of the species. But I know that, as often happens abroad when we encounter the things of home in unfamiliar surroundings, they brought to a head certain obscure impressions that had long been working in my imagination. I remembered, for instance, the "young instructors" I had encountered between Boston and San Francisco; I remembered the sad, sapless air of so many of them and their sepulchral voices, the notes of that essential priggishness the characteristic of which, according to Chesterton, is to have more pride in the possession of one's intellect than joy in the use of it. I fell to thinking about this professor and that I had known at home, and about our intellectual and artistic life in general. How anæmic it seemed, how thin, how deficient in the tang and buoyancy of youth, in personal conviction and impassioned fancy, how lacking in the richer notes! And at last there arose in my mind the memory of a concert at which all the accepted American composers had appeared on the stage one after another, grave, earnest, high-minded, and tinkled out their little intellectual harmonies. Surely, I said to myself again, there is something sadly amiss with our creative life.

Am I wrong in my impression that our "serious" people really are like leaves prematurely detached from the great tree of life? As a class they seem never to have been young, and they seem never to grow mellow and wise. Take our earnest popular novelists off guard; read their occasional comments on society, on the war, even on their own art. How dull, how mechanical, how utterly wanting in fresh insight their minds in general are! Mr. Winston Churchill, expatiating on citizenship, talks in one breath with all the puzzled gravity of a child and some of the weary flatulence of a retired evangelist. Even when they are not evangelical but writers merely they still seem somehow uprooted from the friendly soil. Something infinitely old and disillusioned peers out between the rays of George Ade's wit, and Mrs. Wharton's intellectuality positively freezes the fingers with which one turns her page. And it is the same in our other arts, the plastic arts alone perhaps excepted. Think of that one little vibrant chord, like a naked nerve perpetually harped on, that constitutes the theatrical art of Mrs. Fiske! Think of the arctic frigidity of Mr. Paul Elmer More's criticism! That little seed of the spirit a wayward and unlucky wind has planted in them, why has it never been able to take on flesh and blood, why has it so dried up the springs of animal impulse? It is as if, driven in upon themselves, their lives were a constant strain, as if their emotional natures had run dry and they had come to exist solely in their intellects and their nerves, as if in fact they had gone gray and bloodless precisely in the measure that an inflexible conscience had enabled them in spite of all to trim the little lamp that flickered in them.

Grow they certainly do not. With immense difficulty our intellectual types forge for themselves a point of view with which they confront the world, but like a suit of armor it permits no further expansion. They do not move easily within it; they are chafed and irritated by it; in order to breathe freely they are obliged to hold themselves rigidly to the posture they have at first adopted; and far from being able to de-

velop spontaneously beyond this original posture they have to submit to its cramping limitations until the inevitable shrinkage of their mental tissues brings them release and relief.

Whatever the reason may be, it is certain
that the long-fermented mind, the counselor,
the wise old man of letters, the mind that re-
lates past, present, and future, is a type our
civilization all but utterly fails to produce.
Our thinking class quickly reaches middle age
and after a somewhat prolonged period during
which it seems to be incapable of assimilating
any fresh experiences it begins to decay.   The
rest of our people meanwhile never even grow
up.   For if our old men of thought come to a
standstill at middle age, our old men of action,
as one sees them in offices, in the streets, in public positions, everywhere! are typically not old
men at all but old boys.   Graybeards of sixty
or seventy, mentally and spiritually indistin-
guishable from their sons and grandsons, existing on a level of reflection and emotion in no

way deeper or richer than that of their own childhood, they seem to have miraculously passed through life without undergoing any of life's maturing influences.

III

In short, I think we are driven to the conclusion that our life is, on all its levels, in a state of arrested development, that it has lost, if indeed it has ever possessed, the principle of growth.

To the general sense of this many of the main documents in our recent literature bear witness. Consider, for example, those vast literary pyramids of Mr. Theodore Dreiser, those prodigious piles of language built of the commonest rubble and cohering, in the absence of any architectural design, by sheer virtue of their weight and size. Mr. Dreiser's Titans and Financiers and Geniuses are not even the approximations of men in a world of men,—they are monsters, blindly effectuating themselves, or failing to effectuate themselves, in a primeval chaos; and the world wears them and wearies them as it wears and wearies the beasts of the field, leaving them as immature in age as it found them in youth. Cowperwood, the financier, put in prison as a result of his piratical machinations, weaves chair-bottoms and marks time spiritually against the day of his release, when he snaps back into his old self absolutely unaltered by reflection: and of Eugene Witla, after he has passed through seven hundred and thirty-four pages of soul-searing adventure, Mr. Dreiser is able to enquire: "Was he not changed then? Not much, no. Only hardened intellectually and emotionally, tempered for life and work." Puppets as they are of an insensate force which has never been transmuted into those finer initiatives that shed light on human destiny, they are insulated against human values; love and art pass into and out of their lives like things of so little meaning that any glimmer of material opportunity outshines them; and therefore they are able to speak to us only of the vacuity of life, telling us that human beings are as the flies of summer.

And then there is the *Spoon River Anthology*. The immense and legitimate vogue of this book is due to its unerring diagnosis of what we all recognize, when we are confronted with it, as the inner life of the typical American community when the criterion of humane values is brought to bear upon it in place of the criterion of material values with which we have traditionally pulled the wool over our eyes. It is quite likely of course that Mr. Masters, with a reasonable pessimism, has exaggerated the suicidal and murderous tendencies of the Spoon Riverites. But I know that he conveys an extraordinarily just and logical impression. He pictures a community of some thousands of souls every one of whom lives in a spiritual isolation as absolute as that of any lone farmer on the barren prairie, a community that has been utterly unable to spin any sort of spiritual fabric common to all, which has for so many generations cherished and cultivated its animosity toward all those non-utilitarian elements in the human heart that retard the successful pursuit of the main chance that it has reduced itself to a spiritual desert in which nothing humane is able to find rootage and grow at all.   And yet all the types that shed glory on humankind have existed in that, as in every community! They have existed, or at least they have been born.   They have put forth one green shoot only to wither and decay because all the moisture has evaporated out of the atmosphere that envelops them.   Poets, painters, philosophers, men of science and religion, are all to be found, stunted, starved, thwarted, embittered, prevented from taking even the first step in self-development, in this amazing microcosm of our society, a society that stagnates for want of leadership, and at the same time, incurably suspicious of the very idea of leadership, saps away all those vital elements that produce the leader.

For that is the vicious circle in which we revolve. In the absence both of an intellectual tradition and a sympathetic soil, we who above all peoples need great men and great ideals have been unable to develop the latent greatness we possess and have lost an incalculable measure of greatness that has, in spite of all, succeeded in developing itself. For one thing, we have lost an army of gifted minds, of whom Henry James and Whistler are only the most notorious examples, minds about which our intellectual life could have rallied to its infinite advantage, as it always does when born leaders are in the field.

But the loss, great and continuing as it is, of so many talents that we have repelled and poured out, talents that have been driven to an exotic development in other countries, is really nothing beside what we have lost in ways that are perhaps less obvious. We are the victims of a systematic process of inverse selection so far as the civilizing elements in the American

nature are concerned. Our ancestral faith in
the individual and what he is able to accomplish (or, in modern parlance, to "put over")
as the measure of all things has despoiled us of
that instinctive human reverence for those di-
vine reservoirs of collective experience, religion,
science, art, philosophy, the self-subordinating
service of which is almost the measure of the
highest happiness. In consequence of this our
natural capacities have been dissipated; they
have become ego-centric and socially centrifugal
and they have hardened and become fixed in
the most anomalous forms. The religious energy of the race, instead of being distilled and
quintessentialized into the finer inspirations of
human conduct, has escaped in a vast vapor
that is known under a hundred names. So
also our scientific energy has been diverted from
the study of life to the immediacies of practical
invention, our philosophy, quite forgetting that
its function is to create values of life, has oscil-
lated between a static idealism and a justifica-

tion of all the anæmic tendencies of an anæmic age, and our art and literature, oblivious of the soul of man, have established themselves on a superficial and barren technique.

Of all this individualism is at once the cause and the result. For it has prevented the formation of a collective spiritual life in the absence of which the individual, having nothing greater than himself to subordinate himself to, is either driven into the blind alley of his appetites or rides some hobby of his own invention until it falls to pieces from sheer craziness. Think of the cranks we have produced! Not the mere anonymous cranks one meets, six to a block, in every American village, but the eminent cranks, and even the preëminent cranks, the Thoreaus and Henry Georges, men who might so immensely more have enriched our spiritual heritage had we been capable of assimilating their minds, nurturing and disciplining them out of their aberrant individualism. For every member of the vast army of American cranks has been the graveyard of some "happy thought," some thought happier than his neighbors have had and which has turned sour in his brain because the only world he has known has had no use for it. As for our literature, it is quite plain that there is nothing inherently "greater" in many of the writers whose work we import (and rightly import) from abroad than in writers of a corresponding order at home. The former simply have been able to make a better use of their talents owing to the complicated system of critical and traditional forces perpetually at play about them.

For only where art and thought and science organically share in the vital essential programme of life can the artist and the thinker and the scientist find the preliminary foothold that enables them properly to undertake their task. To state the case in its lowest terms, only under these conditions are they able to receive an adequate, intensive training along non-utilitarian lines without hopelessly crippling their chances of self-preservation; for under these conditions they know that the social fabric is complicated enough to employ all the faculties of their minds and that in following non-utilitarian interests they are fulfilling a recognized need of society. It is this which breeds in them the sense that they are serving something great, something so generally felt to be great that society rewards them with a pride calling forth their own pride, taking delight in setting up the sort of obstacles that constantly put them on their mettle.

Without these conditions we cannot have great leaders; without leaders we cannot have a great society. If this suggests the hope of a "national culture" to come it is only in order that America may be able in the future to give something to the rest of the world that is better than what the world too generally means by "Americanism." For two generations the most sensitive minds in Europe—Renan, Ruskin, Nietzsche, to name none more recent—

have summed up their mistrust of the future in that one word; and it is because, altogether externalized ourselves, we have typified the universally externalizing influences of modern industrialism.   The shame of this is a national shame, and one that the war, with all the wealth it has brought us, has infinitely accentuated.   And it covers a national problem—the problem of creating objects of loyalty within the nation by virtue of which the springs of our creative energy are not only touched into play but so economized as to be able to irrigate the entire subsoil of our national life.

CHAPTER II

THE CULTURE OF INDUSTRIALISM

I

IF we are dreaming of a "national culture" to-day it is because our inherited culture has so utterly failed to meet the exigencies of our life, to seize and fertilize its roots. It is amazing how that fabric of ideas and assumptions, of sentiments and memories and attitudes which made up the civilization of our fathers has melted away like snow uncovering the sordid facts of a society that seems to us now so little advanced on the path of spiritual evolution. The older generation does not recognize its offspring in the crude chaotic manifestations of the present day, but I wonder if it ever considers this universal lapse from grace in the light of cause and effect? I wonder if it ever suspects that there must have been some inherent weakness in a culture that has so lost control of a really well-disposed younger generation, a culture which, after being dominant for so long, has left in its wake a society so little civilized? What is the secret of its decay? And how does it happen that we, whose minds are gradually opening to so many living influences of the past, feel as it were the chill of the grave as we look back over the spiritual history of our own race?

It was the culture of an age of pioneering, the reflex of the spirit of material enterprise—that is the obvious fact; and with the gradual decay of the impulse of enterprise it has itself disintegrated like a mummy at the touch of sunlight. Why? Because it was never a living, active culture, releasing the creative energies of men. Its function was rather to divert these energies, to prevent the anarchical, skeptical, extravagant, dynamic forces of the spirit from taking the wind out of the myth of "progress," that myth imposed by destiny upon the imagination of our forebears in order that a great uncharted continent might be subdued to the service of the race.

For the creative impulses of men are always at war with their possessive impulses, and poetry, as we know, springs from brooding on just those aspects of experience that most retard the swift advance of the acquisitive mind. The spirit of a living culture, which ever has within it some of the acid of Pascal's phrase: "Cæsar was too old to go about conquering the world; he ought to have been more mature"— how could this ever have been permitted to grow up, even supposing that it might have been able to grow up, in a people confronted with forests and prairies and impelled by the necessities of the race to keep their hearts whole and their minds on their task? No, it was essential that everything in men should be repressed

and denied that would have slackened their
manual energy and made their ingenuity a thing
of naught, that would have put questions into
their minds, that would have made them static
materially and dynamic spiritually, that would
have led them to feel too much the disparity
between the inherited civilization they had left
behind and the environment in which they had
placed themselves, that would have neutral-
ized the allure of the exterior ambition which
led them on.

Puritanism was a complete philosophy for
the pioneer and by making human nature con-
temptible and putting to shame the charms of
life it unleashed the acquisitive instincts of men,
disembarrassing those instincts by creating the
belief that the life of the spirit is altogether a
secret life and that the imagination ought never
to conflict with the law of the tribe. It was
this that determined the character of our old
culture, which cleared the decks for practical
action by draining away all the irreconcilable

elements of the American nature into a transcendental upper sphere.

European critics have never been able to understand why a "young nation," living a vigorous, primitive life, should not have expressed itself artistically in a cognate form; and because Whitman did so they accepted him as the representative poet of America. So he was; but it is only now, long after the pioneer epoch has passed and the "free note" has begun to make itself heard, that he has come to seem a typical figure to his own countrypeople. In his own time Whitman was regarded with distrust and even hatred because, by releasing, or tending to release, the creative faculties of the American mind, by exacting a poetical coöperation from his readers, he broke the pioneer law of self-preservation. By awakening people to their environment, by turning democracy from a fact into a spiritual principle, his influence ran directly counter to the necessities of the age, and his fellow-writers justly shunned him for hitting in this way below the belt. In fact, had Whitman continued to develop along the path he originally marked out for himself he might have seriously interfered with the logical process of the country's material evolution. But there was in Whitman himself a large share of the naïve pioneer nature, which made it impossible for him to take experience very seriously or to develop beyond a certain point. As he grew older, the sensuality of his nature led him astray in a vast satisfaction with material facts, before which he purred like a cat by the warm fire. This accounts for the reconciliation which occurred in later years between Whitman and his literary contemporaries. They saw that he had become harmless; they accepted him as a man of talent; and making the most of his more conventional verse, they at last crowned him provisionally as the "good gray poet."

For the orthodox writers of the old school had a serious duty to perform in speeding the

pioneers on their way; and they performed it
with an efficiency that won them the gratitude
of all their contemporaries.   Longfellow with
his lullabies, crooning to sleep the insatiable
creative appetites of the soul, Lowell, with his
"weak-wing'd song" exalting "the deed"—how
invaluable their literature was to the "tired
pioneer," forerunner of the "tired business man"
of the present day and only a loftier type because, like the tired soldier of the trenches, it
was in response to the necessities of the race
that he had dammed at their source the reju-
venating springs of the spirit! Yes, it was a
great service those old writers rendered to the
progress of this country's primitive development, for by unconsciously taking in charge,
as it were, all the difficult elements of human
nature and putting them under an anæsthesia,
they provided a free channel for the *élan* of
their age.

But in so doing they shelved our spiritual
life, conventionalizing it in a sphere above the

sphere of action.   In happier countries literature is the vehicle of ideals and attitudes that
have sprung from experience, ideals and attitudes that release the creative impulses of the
individual and stimulate a reaction in the individual against his environment.   This our
literature has failed to do; it has necessarily remained an exercise rather than an expression.
Itself denied the principle of life or the power
of giving life, it has made up for its failure to
motivate the American scene and impregnate
it with meaning by concentrating all its forces
in the exterior field of æsthetic form.   Gilding
and idealizing everything it has touched and
frequently attaining a high level of imaginative
style, it has thrown veils over the barrenness
and emptiness of our life, putting us in extremely good conceit with ourselves while actually doing nothing either to liberate our minds
or to enlighten us as to the real nature of our
civilization.   Hence we have the meticulous
technique of our contemporary "high-class"

magazines, a technique which, as we know, can be acquired as a trick, and which, artistic as it appears, is really the mark of a complete spiritual conventionality and deceives no sensible person into supposing that our general cleverness is the index of a really civilized society.

II

This total absence of any organic native culture has determined our response to the culture of the outer world. There are no vital relationships that are not reciprocal and only in the measure that we undergo a cognate experience ourselves can we share in the experience of others. To the Catholic, Dante, to the aristocrat, Nietzsche, to the democrat, Whitman, inevitably means more than any of them can mean to the scholar who merely receives them all through his intellect without the palpitant response of conviction and a sympathetic experience. Not that this "experience" has to be identical in the literal sense; no, the very essence of being cultivated is to have developed a capacity for sharing points of view other than our own. But there is all the difference between being actively and passively cultivated that there is between living actively or passively emotional lives. Only the creative mind can really apprehend the expressions of the creative mind. And it is because our field of action has been preëmpted by our acquisitive instincts, because in short we have no national fabric of spiritual experience, that we are so unable to-day to think and feel in international terms. Having ever considered it our prerogative to pluck the fruits of the spirit without undergoing the travail of generating them, having ever given to the tragi-comedy of the creative life a notional rather than a real assent, to quote Newman's famous phrase, we have been able to feed ourselves with the sugar-coating of all the bitter pills of the rest of mankind, accepting the achievements of their creative life as effects which presuppose in us no causal relationships. That is why we are so terribly at ease in the Zion of world culture.

All this explains the ascendancy among our fathers of the Arnoldian doctrine about "knowing the best that has been thought and said in the world." For, wrapped up as they were in their material tasks, it enabled them to share vicariously in the heritage of civilization, endowing them, as it were, with all the pearls of the oyster while neatly evading in their behalf the sad responsibility of the oyster itself. It upholstered their lives with everything that is best in history, with all mankind's most sumptuous effects quite sanitarily purged of their ugly and awkward organic relationships. It set side by side in the Elysian calm of their bookshelves all the warring works of the mighty ones of the past. It made the creative life synonymous in their minds with finished things, things that repeat their message over and over and "stay put." In short, it conventionalized for them the spiritual experience of humanity, pigeonholing it, as it were, and leaving them fancy-free to live "for practical purposes."

I remember that when as children we first read Carlyle and Ruskin we were extremely puzzled by their notes of exasperated indignation. "What are they so angry about?" we wondered, and we decided that England must be a very wicked country. Presently, however, even this idea passed out of our heads, and we came to the conclusion that anger and indignation must be simply normal properties of the literary mind (as they are, in a measure) and that we ought to be grateful for this because they produce so many engaging grotesqueries of style. Our own life was so obviously ship-shape and water-tight—was it possible that people in other countries could have allowed their life to become less so? Unable as we were to decide this point, we were quite willing to give the prophets the benefit of the doubt, as regards their own people. But it was inconceivable that for us they meant any more by their emotional somersaults than the prophets of the Bible meant, whose admirably intoned objurgations we drank in with perfect composure on Sundays.

How natural, then, that the greatest, the most "difficult" European writers should have had, as Carlyle and Browning and Meredith had, their first vogue in America! How natural that we should have flocked about Ibsen, patronized Nietzsche, found something entertaining in every kind of revolutionist, and welcomed the strangest philosophies (the true quite as readily as the false)! For having ourselves undergone no kindred creative experience for them to corroborate and extend, we have ever been able to escape their slings and arrows with a whole skin. They have said nothing real to us because there has been nothing in our own field of reality to make their messages real.

Consequently, those very European writers who might, under normal circumstances, have done the most to shake us out of our compla-

cency have only served the more to confirm us
in it. Our immediate sphere of action being
sealed against them, their influence has been
deflected into "mere literature," where it has
not been actually inverted. For in so far as
our spiritual appetites have been awake, it has
only gone to convince us, not that we are un-
enlightened ourselves, but that other people are
wicked. This explains the double paradox that
while our reformers never consider it necessary
to take themselves in hand before they set out
to improve the world, our orthodox literary men,
no matter what models they place before themselves, cannot rise above the tribal view of their
art as either an amusement or a soporific.

III

How then can our literature be anything but
impotent? It is inevitably so, since it springs
from a national mind that has been sealed
against that experience from which literature
derives all its values.

How true this is can be seen from almost any of its enunciations of principle, especially on the popular, that is to say the frankest, level. I open, for instance, one of our so-called better-class magazines and fall upon a character-sketch of William Gillette: "What a word! *Forget!* What a feat! What a faculty! Lucky the man who can himself forget. How gifted the one who can make others forget. It is the triumph of the art of William Gillette that in the magic of his spell an audience forgets." Opening another magazine I turn to a reported interview in which a well-known popular poet expatiates on his craft. "Modern life," he tells us, "is full of problems, complex and difficult, and the man who concentrates his mind on his problems all day doesn't want to concentrate it on tediously obscure poetry at night. The newspaper poets are forever preaching the sanest optimism, designed for the people who really need the influence of optimism—the breadwinners, the weary, the heavy-laden. That's the kind of poetry the people want, and the fact that they want it shows that their hearts and heads are all right."

Here are two typical pronouncements of the American mind, one on the art of acting, one on the art of poetry, and they unite in expressing a perfectly coherent doctrine. This doctrine is that the function of art is to turn aside the problems of life from the current of emotional experience and create in its audience a condition of cheerfulness that is not organically derived from experience but added from the outside. It assumes that experience is not the stuff of life but something essentially meaningless; and not merely meaningless but an obstruction which retards and complicates our real business of getting on in the world and getting up in the world, and which must therefore be ignored and forgotten and evaded and beaten down by every means in our power.

What is true on the popular level is not less true on the level of serious literature, in spite of everything our most conscientious artists have been able to do. Thirty years ago an acute English critic remarked, apropos of a novel by Mr. Howells, that our novelists seemed to regard the Civil War as an occurrence that separated lovers, not as something that ought normally to have colored men's whole thoughts on life. And it is true that if we did not know how much our literature has to be discounted, we could hardly escape the impression, for all the documents which have come down to us, that our grandfathers really did pass through the war without undergoing the purgation of soul that is often said to justify the workings of tragic mischance in human affairs. Mr. Howells has himself given us the *comédie humaine* of our post-bellum society, Mr. Howells whose whole aim was to measure the human scope of that society and who certainly far less than any other novelist of his time falsified his vision of reality in the interests of popular entertainment. Well, we know the sort of so-

ciety Mr. Howells pictured and how he pictured
it.   He has himself explicitly stated, in connec-
tion with certain Russian novels, that Americans in general do not undergo the varieties of
experience that Russian fiction records, that
"the more smiling aspects of life" are "the
more American," and that in being true to our
"well-to-do actualities" the American novelist
does all that can be expected of him.   Could
one ask for a more essential declaration of artistic bankruptcy than that?

For what does it amount to, this declaration?
It identifies the reality of the artist's vision
with what is accepted as reality in the world
about him.   But every one knows that the
sketchiest, the most immature, the most trivial
society is just as susceptible as any other of the
most profound artistic reconstruction; all that
is required is an artist capable of penetrating
beneath it.   The great artist floats the visible
world on the sea of his imagination and measures it not according to its own scale of values

but according to the values that he has himself derived from his descent into the abysses of life. What, then, is amiss with our writers? They are victims of the universal taboo which the ideal of material success, of the acquisitive life, has placed upon experience. It matters not at all that they have no part or lot in this ideal, that they are men of the finest artistic conscience. In the first place, from their earliest childhood they are taught to repress everything that conflicts with the material welfare of their environment; in the second place, their environment is itself so denatured, so stripped of everything that might nourish the imagination, that they do not so much mature at all as externalize themselves in a world of externalities. Unable to achieve a sufficiently active consciousness of themselves to return upon their environment and overthrow it and dissolve it and recreate it in the terms of a personal vision, they gradually come to accept it on its own terms. If Boston is their theme, they become Bos-

tonian; if it is the Yukon, they become "abys-
mal brutes"; if it is nature, nature becomes
the hero of their work; and if it is machinery,
the machines themselves become vocal and express their natural contempt for a humanity
that is incapable, either morally or artistically,
of putting them in their place and keeping them
there.

We know how this occurred with Mr. Howells. "It seemed to me then, and for a good
while afterward," he writes in *Literary Friends
and Acquaintance*, apropos of his first recep-
tion by the Boston Olympians of the sixties,
"that a person who had seen the men and had
the things said before him that I had in Boston,
could not keep himself too carefully in cotton;
and this was what I did all the following win-
ter, though of course it was a secret between
me and me." Never, assuredly, in any other
society, has literary hero-worship taken quite
the complexion of that; for the statement is
accurately true. Such was the prestige of

Boston and the pundits of Boston that Mr. Howells, having cast his anchor in its lee, never felt the necessity of exploring, on his own account, beyond the spacious, quiet harbor of life that presented itself to the cultivated New England eye. The result can be seen in such novels as *A Modern Instance*, the tragedy of which is viewed not from the angle of an experience that is wider and deeper, as the experience of a great novelist always is, than that of any character the novelist's imagination is able to conceive, but from the angle of Ben Halleck, the epitome of Boston's best public opinion. Boston passes judgment, and Mr. Howells concurs; and you close the book feeling that you have seen life not through the eye of a free personality but of a highly conventional community at a given epoch.

It is exactly the same, to ignore a thousand incidental distinctions, in the work of Jack London. Between the superman of European fiction and Jack London's superman there is all the difference that separates an ideal achieved in the mind of the writer and a fact accepted from the world outside him; all the difference, in short, that separates the truth of art from the appearance of life. If these, therefore, among the freshest and most original talents our fiction has known since Hawthorne's day, have been absorbed in an atmosphere which no one has ever been able to condense, is it remarkable that the rank and file have slipped and fallen, that they have never learned to stand upright and possess themselves? Is it remarkable that they sell themselves out at the first bid, that they dress out their souls in the ready-made clothes the world offers them?

Such, in fact, is the deficiency of personal impulse, of the creative will, in America, so overwhelming is the demand laid upon Americans to serve ulterior and impersonal ends, that it is as if the springs of spiritual action had altogether evaporated. Launched in a society where individuals and their faculties appear only to pass away, almost wholly apart from and without acting upon one another, our writters find themselves enveloped in an impalpable atmosphere that acts as a perpetual dissolvent to the whole field of reality both within and without themselves, an atmosphere that invades every sphere of life and takes its discount from everything that they can do, an atmosphere that prevents the formation of oases of reality in the universal chaos.   Is it remarkable that they take refuge in the abstract, the non-human, the impersonal, in the "bigness" of the phenomenal world, in the surface values of "local color," and in the "social conscience," which enables them to do so much good by writing badly that they often come to think of artistic truth itself as an enemy of progress?

IV

Thus, because it possesses none of those values which endow life with a significance in and of itself, values which art and literature alone can give, the American mind has been gradually subdued to what it has worked in. It has had no barriers to throw up against the overwhelming material forces that have beleaguered it. Consequently, it has gone out of itself as it were and assumed the values of its environment.

Of this the most obvious example is the peculiar optimism, the so-called systematic optimism, that can be fairly taken as what psychologists call the "total reaction upon life" of the typical American mind of the last twenty years. Mr. Horace Fletcher has defined this optimism in terms that leave no doubt of its being at once an effect and a cause of our spiritual impotence:

"Optimism can be prescribed and applied as a medicine. Is there anything new and practical in this or is it but a continuation of the endless discussion of the philosophy of life, morals, medicine, etc.? Is it something that a busy person may put into practice, take with him to his business, without interfering with his business, and profit by; and, finally, what does it cost?   Does adoption of it involve discharging one's doctor-friend, displeasing one's pastor, alienating one's social companions, or shocking the sacred traditions that were dear to father and mother?   It is ameliorative, preventive, and harmonizing; and also it is easy, agreeable, ever available, and altogether profitable.   By these hall-marks of Truth we know that it is true."

Grotesque as this may seem, you will search in vain for a more accurate presentation of the workaday point of view of our tumbling American world.   This is the way Americans think, and what they think, whether they profess the religion of mind cure, uplift, sunshine, popular pragmatism, the gospel of advertising, or plain business; and they mean exactly what the beauty experts mean when they say, "Avoid strong emotions if you wish to retain a youthful complexion."   Systematic optimism, in other words, effects a complete revaluation of values and enthrones truth upon a conception of animal success the prerequisite of which is a thorough-going denial and evasion of emotional experience.   It is the chronic result of contact with a prodigal nature too easily borne under by a too great excess of will, of opportunities so abundant and so alluring that we have been led to suppress the creative spirit in ourselves, traditionally unaware as we are of the mature potentialities and justifications of human nature, and establish our scale of values in the incomparably rich material territory that surrounds us.   If to-day, therefore, we find no principle of integrity at work in any department of our life, if religion competes with advertising, art competes with trade, and trade gives itself out as philanthropy, if we present to the world at large the spectacle of a vast undifferentiated herd of good-humored animals, it is because we have passively surrendered our human values at the demand of circumstance.

CHAPTER III

YOUNG AMERICA

"When first hatched they are free-swimming micro-
scopic creatures, but in a few hours they fall to the
bottom and are lost unless they can adhere to a firm,
clean surface while making their shells and undergoing development."

—*Report on the Oyster Industry.*

WHEN I speak of the culture of industrialism
I do not mean to imply that it has been peculiar
to us. Everywhere the industrial process has
devitalized men and produced a poor quality of
human nature. By virtue of this process the
culture of the whole Western world fell too
largely, during the nineteenth century, into the
hands of the prig and the æsthete, those two sick
blossoms of the same sapless stalk, whose
roots have been for so long unwatered by

the convictions of the race. But in Europe the great traditional culture, the culture that has ever held up the flame of the human spirit, has never been quite gutted out. The industrialism that bowled us over, because for generations our powers of resistance had been undermined by Puritanism, was no sooner well under way in Europe than human nature began to get its back up, so to speak; and a long line of great rebels reacted violently against its desiccating influences. Philologists like Nietzsche and Renan, digging among the roots of Greek and Semitic thought, artists like Morris and Rodin, rediscovering the beautiful and happy art of the Middle Ages, economists like Marx and Mill, revolting against the facts of their environment, kept alive the tradition of a great society and great ways of living and thus were able to assimilate for human uses the positive by-products of industrialism itself, science and democracy. They made it impossible for men to forget the degradation of society and

the poverty of their lives and built a bridge between the greatness of the few in the past and
the greatness of the many, perhaps, in the future. Thus the democracies of Europe are
richer than ours in self-knowledge, possessing
ideals grounded in their own field of reality and
so providing them with a constant stimulus to
rise above their dead selves, never doubting
that experience itself is worth having lived for,
even if it leads to nothing else. And thus,
however slowly they advance, they advance on
firm ground.

For us, individually and socially, as I have
tried to show, nothing of this kind has been possible. It seems to me wonderfully symbolic of
our society that the only son of Lincoln should
have become the president of the Pullman Company, that the son of the man who liberated the
slaves politically should have been the first, as
The Nation pointed out not long ago, to exploit
them industrially. Our disbelief in experience,
our habitual repression of the creative instinct,

our consequent over-stimulation of the acquisitive instinct, has made it impossible for us to
take advantage of the treasures our own life
has yielded. Democracy and science, for example, have *happened to us* abundantly, more
abundantly perhaps than to others because they
have had less inertia to overcome; but like children presented with shining gold pieces we have
not known how to use them. Either we have
been unable to distinguish them from copper
pennies, or else we have spent them in foolish
ways that have made us ill. Our personal life
has in no way contributed to the enriching of
our environment; our environment, in turn, has
given us personally no sense of the significance
of life.

We of the younger generation, therefore, find
ourselves in a grave predicament. For having,
unlike Europeans of any class, no fund of spiritual experience in our blood as it were, to bal-
ance the various parts of our natures, we are
all but incapable of coördinating ourselves in

a free world. We are no longer able to make the sort of "go" of life our fathers made: the whole spirit of our age is against the dualism which they accepted as a matter of course. The acquisitive life has lost the sanction of necessity which the age of pioneering gave it. A new age has begun, an age of intensive cultivation, and it is the creative life that the nation calls for now. But for that how ill-equipped we are! Our literature has prepared no pathways for us, our leaders are themselves lost. We are like explorers who, in the morning of their lives, have deserted the hearthstone of the human tradition and have set out for a distant treasure that has turned to dust in their hands; but having on their way neglected to mark their track they no longer know in which direction their home lies, nor how to reach it, and so they wander in the wilderness, consumed with a double consciousness of waste and impotence.

I think this fairly describes the frame of

mind of a vast number of Americans of the
younger generation. They find themselves born
into a race that has drained away all its spiritual resources in the struggle to survive and
that continues to struggle in the midst of plenty
because life itself no longer possesses any other
meaning. The gradual commercialization of
all the professions, meanwhile, has all but en-
tirely destroyed the possibility of personal
growth along the lines that our society provides
and, having provided, sanctions. Brought up
as they have been to associate activity almost
solely with material ends and unable in this
overwhelmingly prosperous age to feel any pow-
erful incentive to seek these ends, acutely conscious of their spiritual unemployment and impoverished in will and impulse, the more sensitive minds of the younger generation drift
almost inevitably into a state of internal anarchism that finds outlet, where it finds outlet
at all, in a hundred unproductive forms.

Our society, in fact, which does everything

by wholesale, is rapidly breeding a race of Hamlets the like of which has hardly been seen before, except perhaps in nineteenth-century Russia. Nothing is more remarkable than the similarity in this respect between the two immense inchoate populations that flank Europe on east and west. To be sure, the Oblomovs and Bazarovs and Levins and Dmitri Rudins of Russian fiction are in many ways, like Hamlet himself, universal characters. But for one Hamlet in an organized society which, according to the measure of its organization, provides an outlet for every talent, there are twenty in a society which, as we say, has no use for its highly developed types. And that is the situation both in Russia and the United States: the social fabric is too simple to be able to cope with the complicated strain that has been suddenly put upon it by a radical change in the conditions of life. Yet in each case the complexities have developed along just the lines most necessary for the rounded well-being of society. The

Hamlets of Russian fiction, generally speaking, are social idealists, wrapped up in dreams of agricultural and educational reform; they long to revolutionize their country estates and ameliorate the lot of their peasantry, and they lose their will and their vision because there is no social machinery they can avail themselves of: thrown as they are upon their own unaided resources, their task overwhelms them at the outset with a sense of futility.   Turn the tables about and you have the situation of the corresponding class in America.   They find the machinery of education and social welfare in a state as highly developed as the life of the spirit is in Russia; it is the spiritual technique that is wanting, a living culture, a complicated scheme of ideal objectives, upheld by society at large, enabling them to submerge their liberties in their loyalties and to unite in the task of building up a civilization.

In short, owing to the miraculous rapidity and efficiency with which we have been able to effect the material conquest of the continent, a prodigious amount of energy has been thrown out of employment which our society is unable to receive and set to work. All the innate spirituality of the American nature, dammed up, stagnant from disuse, has begun to pour itself out in a vast flood of undisciplined emotionalism that goes—how often!—to waste. It goes to waste largely because the scope of our "useful" objectives is so restricted, and because, inheriting as we do an ingrained individualism, an ingrained belief in quick returns, we are all but unable to retain these treacherous elements, of which we have had so little practical experience in the past, until they have reached a sufficient maturity to take shape in lasting forms.

But this new individualism, which finds its gospel in self-expression, is totally different from the individualism of the past. The old spiritual individualism was blood-brother to the old materialistic individualism: it throve in the same soil and produced a cognate type of mind.

It was hard, stiff-necked, combative, opiniona-
tive, sectarian, self-willed; it gave birth to the
crank, the shrill, high-strung propounder of
strange religions, the self-important monopolist
of truth.   In short, it was essentially competitive.   The new individualism, on the other
hand, is individualistic only by default; its individualistic character, so to say, is only an inherited bad habit, a bad habit that is perpetuated by the want of objectives in the truly
vacuous world with which it finds itself confronted.   It has, I think, no desire to vaunt itself; it tends, instead of this, to lavish itself;
it is not combative, it is coöperative, not opin-
ionative but groping, not sectarian but filled
with an intense, confused eagerness to identify
itself with the life of the whole people.   If it
remains confused, if it is unable to discipline
itself, if it is often lazy and wilful, if its smoke
is only at intervals illuminated by flame—well,
was it not just so with the Oblomovs of Russia?   I can't conceive that any one *wants* to

be confused and lazy, especially if he has no material motives to console him in other ways. People who do not "burn with a hard, gem-like flame" are simply people who are not being employed by civilization.

Undoubtedly the gospel of self-expression, makeshift as it is, has revealed a promise in America that we have always taken for granted but hardly reckoned with. Isolated, secretive, bottled up as we have been in the past, how could we ever have guessed what aims and hopes we have in common had they not been brought to light, even in the crudest and most inadequate ways? That they have at last been brought to light I think few will deny; but will they get any further? Only, it seems to me, if we are able to build up, to adapt a phrase from the slang of politics, a programme for the conservation of our spiritual resources.

"Humanity," wrote Mazzini in 1858, "is a great army marching to the conquest of unknown lands, against enemies both strong and cunning. The peoples are its corps, each with its special operation to carry out, and the common victory depends on the exactness with which they execute the different operations." That nationalities are the workshops of humanity, that each nationality has a special duty to perform, a special genius to exert, a special gift to contribute to the general stock of civilization, and that each, in consequence, growing by the trust that other nationalities place in it, must be a living, homogeneous entity, with its own faith and consciousness of self—could any idea more perfectly than this express the dream, the necessity, of Young America? To live creatively, to live completely, to live in behalf of some great corporate purpose,—that is its desire. A national faith we had once, a national dream, the dream of the "great American experiment." But had it not been sadly compromised would the younger generation find itself adrift as it is to-day? Too many elements of that old faith of ours were at war with all that was good in it, and it admitted so few of the factors of life; it was betrayed by what was false within; it was unable to embrace the freer impulses of a new time. That is why it contributes so little to the new faith without which America cannot live, and for which it now seeks in the darkness of the war.

To discover that faith, to formulate that new technique, to build up, as I have said, that programme for the conservation of our spiritual resources, is the task of criticism and philosophy. Our critics and philosophers, I think, have thus far shirked this task. Why, and in what degree, I hope to suggest in the following chapters.

CHAPTER IV

OUR CRITICS

In a famous essay Matthew Arnold said that it is "the business of the critical power to see the object as in itself it really is." If any of our critics had been able to act upon this principle, if they had been able to put aside their prepossessions and merely open their minds to the facts of American life, even without attempting any of the more heroic measures our life notoriously demands, I think the predicament of the younger generation would be far less grave than it is. For, as Arnold goes on to say, by seeing the object as in itself it really is, criticism "tends to make an intellectual situation of which the creative power can profitably avail itself." There, surely is the very thing that Young America needs. Deficient as it is in creative power, it has more creative desire than it knows what to do with; and is it not a situation of which it can profitably avail itself that turns desire into power? If our critics have failed to make that situation, they can hardly hold Young America responsible for the chaos that now debilitates it. The responsibility, I think, lies rather upon our critics themselves.

For the truth is that, far from "seeing the object as in itself it really is," our critics do not see the object, for them the supreme object, America, the living creative life of America, at all. That is only natural perhaps in the pundits of our criticism, Mr. Paul Elmer More and Professor Irving Babbitt, for example, who feel that there is nothing worth seeing in a world Rousseau has debauched. And perhaps it is not surprising in such sensitive minds of the older generation as Mr. Brownell and Mr. Woodberry, who responded so passionately in their youth to visions of grace that never could have been ours, that they have no heart for the homelier tasks of America.   But, remarkably, it is just as true of those more complacent and sometimes all too complacent critics of the middle generation who feel themselves in life apparently by no means alien to the stirring American scene.   Professor Stuart P. Sherman carries on a guerrilla warfare with his younger contemporaries, but has he ever displayed anything that could be called an interest in them or any desire to find out what they are seeking?   Professor William Lyon Phelps, on the other hand, pats them on the back, but he never dreams of applying values to them because he is romantically anxious *not* to see them as in themselves they really are: he is afraid perhaps to find that they are not the good fellows in print that he likes to think them in life.   As for Mr. J. E. Spingarn, that freest of amateurs, that patron of æsthetic radicalism, he wraps himself in a web of critical theory from which he has never emerged at all into the mêlée of our creative life.   Interest, in short, mere friendly interest, for severe interest we cannot expect, is the last boon our critics yield us. Is it strange, then, that our creative life halts and stammers in bewilderment?

It is certainly remarkable, this apparently general determination not to be practical on the part of so many dissimilar minds; and it is all the more remarkable because criticism has ever been, in other countries, precisely the most practical of the literary arts. Since the days when Socrates, its august founder, sat in the market-place and played the midwife to so many inarticulate minds, it has been the joyous prerogative of criticism to be on the spot when thoughts are being born. Not to mention any names that the most academic of our critics can possibly gainsay, is it not the glory of Lessing that he established a sort of norm of the German character, descending into the thick of reality and building, by creation and controversy alike, amid the shifting sands of pedantry and exoticism, an impregnable base for the superstructure of a civilization to come? As for Sainte-Beuve, he lived in an age and a society that required no such drastic re-statements of fundamental truth; he inherited and perpetuated that marvelous equilibrium of the French temper which is the result of an organic culture founded on the suffrages of the whole race; but Sainte-Beuve lived and wrote in substantial harmony with the creative life of his contemporaries, and he too was ever ready to spring to the defence of new-born thoughts and fight for their just rights of passage into the French mind. No doubt in the France of Sainte-Beuve there were more new-born thoughts worth fighting for, strictly as thoughts, than there are in the America of to-day. But no one denies that at present in this country an immense amount of creative energy has at least conclusively turned itself toward the field of the arts. If it does not in many instances come rightly and fully to a head, if it fails

very often to eventuate in thoughts in themselves vitally important, does it not all the more
behoove criticism to condense the vapors that
confuse this creative energy and to spring loy-
ally to the support of groping minds that bear
the mark of sincerity and promise? As for our
critics, what birth out of life have any of them
ever defended with that heavy artillery they
so enjoy training upon those popular American
fallacies many of which, quite plainly, are the
result of their own immemorial absentee-mind-
edness? Have they ever been at pains to grasp
the contemporary American mind and its problems, to discover what the contemporary American mind is, and what it is capable of, and
how it can best be approached, and whether
it is able to assimilate the whole culture of the
world before it has formed any personal conception of what culture is?

Our critics, if they are in touch with European life, must be aware that the relation in
which they stand to the life of their own coun-

try is quite unique. But far even from considering the idea that the living forces about them deserve a little sympathetic and discreet attention they seem to be persuaded that the younger generation presents a united front against everything that mankind has tried and found worthy, and that it has formed a sort of conspiracy to propagate falsehood at whatever cost. "What Matthew Arnold would call 'the elephantine main body,' " says Mr. Babbitt, "seems more convinced than ever that man, to become perfect, has only to continue indefinitely the programme of the nineteenth century,—that is, to engage in miscellaneous expansion and back it up if need be with noisy revolt against all the forms of the past." To which Mr. Brownell subjoins the following: "Every one who sympathetically 'belongs' to [the age] feels himself stanchly supported by the consensus of all it esteems. . . . The militancy of the age therefore finds itself not only in possession of a perfectly definite—if mainly destructive—

credo, but of a practically united and enthusiastic army."

To us who are so much in the thick of things
that we cannot see the forest for the trees,
statements of this kind are all but unintelligible.
They seem to us like anathemas delivered in
some half-forgotten sacred language to a people that has begun to stammer in a vernacular
of its own. We are so conscious of our own
differences, of the hundred and one programmes
that we are pursuing precisely *not* in common,
that while we are prepared for body-blows from
Mr. Babbitt (to whose vigorous intellect, by the
way, many of us are greatly indebted), we
scarcely know what to make of Mr. Brownell's
rather more graciously delivered thrusts. But
we may be very sure that if, to the older generation, we appear to be a "practically united
and enthusiastic army" we must be so in some
sense in which the older generation is not. To
what that sense is our critics themselves in a
general way have given us the clue. They say

that we are emotional, and they give to their accusation an air of plausibility by adding that we are over-emotional, as indeed we are; but what they really object to is that we are emotional at all, the strength of their own case resting wholly on the assumption that literature ought to spring not from the emotions but from the intellect. This we deny, and I suppose that our denial is so unanimous that it does, in a way, neutralize our intellectual differences. But why do we deny it? Partly because our reaction upon life, on the one hand, and our reading of the history of literature, on the other, leads us to believe that it is false; and partly because we have witnessed the failure and breakdown of intellectualism itself.

Consider, for example, Mr. More, our chief exponent of the intellectualist position. Mr. More, referring to the yellow press, delivers himself of the following remarks: "On days when no sensational event has occurred, it will indulge in the prettiest sentimental sermons on the home and on family felicities. . . . But let the popular mind be excited by some crime of lust, and the same journal will forget the sweet obligations of home and wife . . . and will deck out the loathsome debauchery of a murderer and his trull as the spiritual history of two young souls finding themselves in the pure air of passion." . . . Now, really, whatever the provocations of the yellow press, can one imagine a piece of worse literary breeding than this? Yet it can almost be called Mr. More's habitual tone whenever, leaving the charmed circle of literary ideas, he deals with modern society. Far from being reasonable, disinterested, and humane, his note is one of nagging, pettish, and one would almost say vulgar exasperation; he betrays a tendency to break out on every occasion into promiscuous abuse. How then can our intellectualists expect to convert us to the music of the classical discipline when some of their own most representative minds—for Mr. More is by no means unique as an advocate of "the classic point of view"—are so singularly ill-nurtured? If this is what the classical discipline does—how can we avoid being led, quite unjustly, to conclude?—let us by all means turn to the discipline of science which produced the ever just and ever genial William James.

That is what we mean when we speak of the breakdown of intellectualism; for of course the reason why Mr. More's humane attitude cracks and crumbles so at the touch of life is because it is based on a culture of the intellect that is not borne out by a corresponding culture of the feelings. Mr. More's emotional life, as his writings exhibit it, is just as crude and untempered as the intellectual life of the younger generation which he attacks. Why is this so? Because Mr. More's intellectualism is the converse and counterpart of the materialism that has led to the younger generation's incapacity to accept the discipline he offers it. He has not been able to feel human values finely because to have done so would have been to upset his whole faith in a society based not upon the creative but upon the acquisitive instincts of men, a society ruled over by the "natural aristocracy" of economic power. Mr. More is simply a belated pioneer, with all the repressed impulses, the fundamental limitations, the exaggerated antipathies that belong to the pioneer type, extended and subtilized in the sphere of the intellect alone. Turn from his philosophical and literary essays, in which he is able to be humane at large, to his essays on social and economic themes, and see how quickly he lets the cat out of the bag. "Looking at the larger good of society," he observes, "we may say that the dollar is more than the man and that *the rights of property are more important than the right to life.*"

Here, then, we have a clue not merely to the breakdown of the intellectualist point of view but to its origin as well. Mr. Brownell says that we used to have in this country a public comparable with those *honnêtes gens*, equally removed from a court that was too rigid and a pit that was too free, through which the French tradition was so long maintained. "A public like this," he says, "we once had, and we have it no longer. Its limitations were marked, but they emphasized its existence. Its standards were narrow, but it had standards. We had a class, not numerous but fairly defined, corresponding to the class Charles Sumner found in England, distinct from the nobility but possessed in abundance of serious knowledge, high accomplishment, and refined taste, the class, precisely, called by Molière *les honnêtes gens*." Now, that such a class did exist at one time in this country no one who has any associations with our past could possibly deny. But that this class ever at bottom corresponded with the *honnêtes gens* of France one might perhaps be permitted to question, even if M. André Gide, whom Mr. Brownell quotes from, had not remarked that in France itself the tradition they maintained would hardly have been possible without the court. But why did the existence of the court make so much difference? Because the court, removed as it was from the influences of the market-place, kept alive in France the free, the non-acquisitive, in short the creative conception of life; and this conception, permeating thence downward the whole fabric of society, linked the artistic expressions at the top with the common consciousness of the race beneath, a common consciousness that has never denied its Rabelaisian elements. Between these two extremes, then, of racial experience and racial expression and partaking abundantly of both, the *honnêtes gens*, with their "serious knowledge, their high accomplishment, their refined taste" formed a sort of mean, logically poised. French wit, French elegance, French taste—are they not, as Mr. Brownell himself would be the first to point out, simply the polished outside, the polished extremity, as it were, of a social mass that is modeled and civilized all the way through, according to its own genius, a social mass all the strata of which are fused and unified and which is grounded imperturbably on the basis of a common experience of life? It is quite true, as Mr. Brownell says, that Molière would never have written his best work had he practised only on his cook. But is there not a certain difference between French society and our own in the fact that Molière was able to practise on his cook at all?

For our cultivated class of old never demanded, never assumed the existence of, and never attempted to create, a common ground of experience in the American people. It accepted men as "infinitely repellent particles" and drew them together by projecting a spirit that appealed to their intellect and their will alone and that never conflicted with the full exercise of their instincts of acquisition. Having neither on the one hand "a court that was too rigid" but that would, nevertheless, have preserved the creative conception of life, nor on the other "a pit that was too free" but that would, equally, have kept them in touch with a level of primitive emotional life, our cultivated class with their serious knowledge, their high accomplishment, their refined taste were suspended in the air, so to speak, deprived alike of the creative spark that lifts men above themselves and the animal under-proppings that maintain their contact with rude reality. Our old writers established as a common ground between themselves and their readers either the non-human world of external nature (Thoreau), the world of the will (Emerson), the world of memory and association (Longfellow), the emotion of special causes like abolition or the Civil War (Whittier, Lowell) or of special occasions (Holmes), but never the congruous world of human life in general. They knew that their neighbors and that extended neighborship that constituted their public had no emotional life in common because their ex-

istence on the active plane was a competitive
one; bent as their public was on getting on
individually, how could they admit or cultivate
an inner community as social beings?   Admit
it of course they could not, neither could they
cultivate it; and the result was that our old
culture never was and never became organic;—
a by-product of the conditions of its time, it
was unable to project itself beyond those conditions.   That is why it strikes one as so futile
when Mr. Brownell pleads for the extension
of taste without taking into consideration the
primitive forces that will have to undergo a
profound transmutation before taste in the organic sense will really be possible to the American public.   *Inorganic* taste we already have
in abundance, and every year, following the
spread of wealth, it increases more and more.
Nowadays a little money and a little training
and a little expert advice enable almost any-
one to possess a "flawless" drawing-room, for
example (especially if he keeps within the safe

circle of the neutral colors). But is it not abundantly evident that this very general attainment of æsthetic taste is quite compatible with an extreme want of taste in other relations of life?

Upon almost all our social relations, in fact, the effect is so obvious of our competitive, non-creative past that, were it not that our critics belong to that competitive, non-creative past and cannot escape from its circle of ideas, it would seem almost wanton of them to accuse the younger generation of having created a chaos which, in truth, they have only become conscious of. Our critics themselves have always said that our society is too incongruous to produce a high social comedy; but why do they draw the line there? Do they not see that "high" literature in any *genre*, literature, I mean, that is based on a complicated social understanding, is all but impossible for us at present, except on a forced and artificial plane? Consider Dr. Crothers, for example. Why are

the essays of Dr. Crothers so self-conscious if
it is not because Dr. Crothers knows perfectly
well that his eighty thousand readers have no
emotional life in common either with him or
with each other, because he does not feel *at
home* with his readers as Charles Lamb felt,
or even as Dr. Holmes felt in his little Harvard
world of the past? They admit, I suppose,
that Dr. Crothers is self-conscious; but why do
they accept with only a gesture of deprecation
the self-consciousness of Dr. Crothers while
they attack in so savage a way the self-consciousness of the younger generation? Because while the self-consciousness of the younger
generation stands for an instinctive drive toward a common understanding on the creative
plane, the self-consciousness of Dr. Crothers,
making no levy upon our creative life, accepts
the pioneer law of self-preservation, in the
scheme of which literature is only a kind of
associational and secondary play of the mind

in a society whose real business is the art of getting on.

Our critics are thus unable to connect at any point with the creative life of the present time because they are precluded from so doing by the entire programme of the epoch in which they were bred. Mr. Babbitt and Mr. Brownell differ from Mr. More in being instinctively humane minds; but they are in implicit agreement with Mr. More's pioneer sociology, none the less; they have simply not filled out their points of view on the economic and psychological sides, and thus, without deliberately repudiating, they ignore the economic and psychological interpretations of life according to which literature is not an entity in itself but one of the manifestations of society. Here is a statement in point from Mr. Babbitt's *New Laokoon:* "Lessing repudiated what was artificial and superficial in the French tradition,—its conventions, and etiquette, and gallantries,—but at the risk of losing a real virtue, viz., the exquisite urbanity that the French at their best had really succeeded in attaining." Mr. Babbitt, you see, implies that literature and society are distinct entities following separate laws.   For only on the assumption that literature is independent of society and not, as Madame de Staël said a hundred years ago, an expression of it, only on the assumption, that is to say, that literature forms a self-sufficient world of its own, is it possible to dream that you can pick out all the plums from the literary pudding and make a nice little particular pie for yourself.   How, indeed, could this "exquisite urbanity" of the French tradition have been anything but exotic in the Berlin of 1760? And how could it possibly have been preserved when those other characteristics of the French tradition, with which it was organically bound up, had been repudiated?   Was it not, in fact, the great work of Lessing, that work not so much of intelligence as of character for which,

according to Goethe, the Germans have so re-
vered his memory, that he purged the German
mind of *all* its exotic elements and grounded its
literature in the firm subsoil of its own nature?
Our critics, to repeat, maintain this peculiar
cosmopolitan eclecticism partly because, not being creative minds, they do not appreciate, as
the creative mind does, the necessary corre-
spondence between expression and experience,
even, if need be, the most limited, merely local,
experience; and partly because by means of it
they are able to prevent literature from coming
into direct contact with a society whose acquisitive, non-creative programme it would immediately upset and destroy.

From that programme our critics of the middle
generation have been unable to liberate themselves. There is Professor Stuart P. Sherman,
for example. Professor Sherman plainly wants
to take part in the creative life of his contemporaries; besides, he is a natural oppositionist
and a vigorous oppositionist we ought to have.

Nothing is more tonic than to be reminded, constantly and aggressively, of the human significance of points of view other than one's own. But Professor Sherman's opposition is sterile, because it lies outside the creative sphere altogether. Talk as he may of humanism, his humanism is avowedly based upon that of Mr. More, author of the damaging statement that "the rights of property are more important than the right to life"; he cannot therefore convey, because he has obviously never experienced, the artistic value of any principle, even the most reactionary one. An innate conviction that experience itself is vain and that the acquisitive instincts have and ought to have the right of way desiccates the mind of the man who might have been Young America's dearest and most stimulating enemy and has led him to write a book that futilizes not merely the contemporary literature with which it deals but all literature whatsoever.

Mr. Spingarn's mind, of course, is of quite

a different order; but he too belongs to the circle of our past. For while he is up to the minute in his critical theory he is the victim of a society which has so abridged and emasculated the *function* of criticism that he is himself unable to generate enough interest in contemporary phenomena to feel it worth his while to bring his critical apparatus into play. It happens, of course, that many of Mr. Spingarn's ideas are intelligent and true. Why then does so much of his writing reduce itself to a thin dialectic, the wheels of which turn round with extraordinary facility but without gathering heat or throwing out light? Because, while his critical point of view is intellectually admirable, it does not represent the *kind* of criticism for which a society in our stage of development offers an adequate opportunity. Mr. Spingarn's æsthetic, as we know, is derived from that of Benedetto Croce and Benedetto Croce, as we also know, conducts in Italy a critical magazine from which a large part of the literary life of his country takes its direction.   This is an aspect of reality just as real as the reality of Benedetto Croce's ideas.   How does it happen, then, that Mr. Spingarn emulates the one without emulating the other?   Obviously because America is not Italy and because, while a theory may be equally true in all countries, what makes a theory effective is the peculiar condition of the given time and place with which it is brought into relationship.   That works of art ought to be judged purely on their own merits and without regard to time and place is, no doubt, perfectly valid as a standard of criticism. But a criticism that employs that standard will never be able to play the effective part in this country that it plays in Italy until our literature has been brought into such an organic relationship with our life that in discussing literary phenomena on their own merits it will also be discussing, by implication, the society of which literary phenomena are the expression.

Thus Mr. Spingarn, modern as he is and deriving his point of view from a field of learning largely untapped by the critics of the older generation, is essentially, so far as America is concerned, in the same boat with Mr. Babbitt and Mr. Brownell. For just as Mr. Spingarn does not see why he should not take over the Italian criticism of Benedetto Croce, so Mr. Babbitt and Mr. Brownell see no reason why they should not take over the principles and methods of French criticism, in spite of the fact that France is the most perfect example of a social organism the modern world knows, the most perfect example, that is to say, of a spontaneous unity in all departments of life. Obviously in a civilization that is based on a traditional common understanding, where literature proceeds through a constant, illuminating reference to known antecedents, where literary values are fixed by an experience in which all have shared, the merest of "merely" literary criticism is implicitly a form of social criticism as well; and by virtue of this it is true of French critics of whatever school that in touching on a given book they write about France, setting in vibration, throwing into relief, a fragment of the racial consciousness itself. How, then, can the principles and methods of French criticism be divorced altogether from the texture of French society? How can they be taken over bodily and applied in societies that possess no comparable organic development? The answer is that they can be taken over but that they can not be applied, as the whole work of our orthodox critics goes to prove; for the classical method loses its force at once when it is brought to bear on a literature that has no values based on experience and expresses no achieved social organism but only the necessarily irresponsible impulses of isolated individuals. Our critics, by assuming this attitude, not in regard to specific works, for these they ignore, but in regard to the tendencies that lie behind them, are led quite naturally to find in these tendencies nothing but sound and fury, signifying nothing.

But they themselves are unable to suggest any principles of order adapted to a spiritually un-organized society.

CHAPTER V

OUR AWAKENERS

I

In that very interesting testament, *Literature in Ireland*, which he left for his fellow-poets, Thomas MacDonagh showed how disadvantageous it is to have a full-grown criticism side by side with what he calls a baby literature. "There is," he says, "a school of criticism in Ireland, a school that knows the work of the finest critics in the world, and knows too, what is more important, the finest literature in the world. This, when dealing with literature in general, adds to the store of fine critical work. This at times encourages and approves good original Irish work. I think it unfortunate, however, that it should have grown with, or indeed before, the original work. Dealing with the monuments of the older literatures—English, French, and the like—this criticism knows its place, its bearings, its conditions. Dealing with a naissant literature it looks over its shoulder, as it were. Its neck is awry. Its eyes are twisted round. Its feet turn from their known way and stumble. When it does get a clear view of its object, it misses the shapes and forms it saw in other lands and expresses its disappointment."

Of our own criticism surely, of our own critics, one could hardly have a better description than that. For Ireland and America really are alike in that they inherit a dominant academic tradition colonial in essence, having its home in centers of civilization remote from the springs of a national life which has only of late come into its own consciousness. For the shaping of that consciousness, therefore, we cannot look to our critics for any assistance. Not guides and friends of the creative spirit about them but incredulous pedagogues by necessity, they have been really driven to destroy

in others the poet that has died in themselves.
Of their "humanism" let this be the merciful
epitaph.

But, after all, our critics have never set up
to be national awakeners. They have never
pretended to be on terms of intimacy with the
real conditions of our life; they know in their
own hearts, I think, that they cannot suggest
any way out of our difficulties. Who, then,
are, or who purport to be, our real awakeners?
The sociologists whose doctrine is the adapta-
tion of man to his environment, the apostles of
a narrow efficiency, and the pragmatic and real-
istic philosophers who stand behind them. For
twenty years and more now they have occupied
the center of our life. They have not only accepted reality, they have claimed reality, they
have said that they alone apprehend reality,
and that reality has been taken out of the hands
of the muddleheads and put in their special
charge because they alone are able to do something with it. Well, and here we are. They

have asked us to judge them by their fruits.
What are we to say?

For the influence of these awakeners of ours
has been, directly or indirectly, universal; their
philosophy has been the formulation, the ra-
tionalization of the whole spirit of American
life at least since the Spanish war. And ob-
serve the condition in which we now are: sul-
try, flaccid, hesitant, not knowing what we want
and incapable of wanting anything very much,
certainly not in love with our life, certainly not
at home in this field of reality our awakeners
have bidden us to be at home in, inclined as
ever to substitute monetary for real values, and
to stand in mortal fear of letting loose the
spiritual appetites that impede our pursuit of
a neat, hygienic, and sterile success. . . .
What, in fact, *is* the note of our society to-
day? A universal tepidity, it seems to me, the
faded offspring of the Puritan hatred of human
nature, which makes perhaps a majority of our
kindly fellow-countrymen seem quite incapable

of living, loving, thinking, dreaming, or hoping with any degree of passion or intensity, pacifistic at bottom not from any specific realization of war but from a distaste for the militant life *in toto*.   We know this only too well; it is the secret of our humiliation, and it explains the desire of so many people to see this country rudely jolted and shaken up; it explains the pathological hopes that so many people lavish upon the war, hopes that have been bred by the morbid state into which we are fallen. . . . What can our awakeners say to all this?   It is not their fault, certainly, that things are so; but so things are, and it is in the days of their consulate that things have become so.   Out of pragmatism our new leadership has been recruited—the leadership of "interpretation."   If at last that leadership has revealed itself as no leadership at all, I think it is because pragmatism, by default, has got itself into a false position.

By default, I say; for not content with remaining a method, it has, owing to the impotence of our poetical tradition and the extra-scientific sympathies of its founders, attempted to fill the place which poetry alone can fill adequately, and which our poetry, in its complacent animalism on the one hand, and its complicated escape from reality on the other, has left vacant. That is to say, it has assumed the right to formulate the aims of life and the values by which those aims are tested, aims and values which, we are led by history to believe, can be effectively formulated only by individual minds not in harmony with the existing fact but in revolt against it. Social efficiency is the ideal posited by Professor Dewey. But an ideal is an end, and social efficiency is not an end; it is a means toward the realization of human values. Has not the purpose, has not even the *scope* of social efficiency ever been determined by individuals who from time to time repudiate the social organism altogether and, rising themselves to a fresh level, drag mankind after them?

Life proceeds not by the burnishing up of exist-
ent ideals, but by the discovery of new and more
vital ones, thanks to the imagination, which
reaches out into an unknown whither the intelligence is able to follow only by a long second.
Does not pragmatism therefore turn the natural
order of things inside out when it accepts the intelligence instead of the imagination as the
value-creating entity?   It does, virtually if not
absolutely, and in so doing crowds out and re-
places the essential factor from which all dynamic creativity springs.   It becomes, in a
word, the dog in the manger of our creative life.
What if it is an amiable, friendly dog with none
of the other disagreeable proclivities of the dog
in the fable?   The main thing is that it makes
its bed where the wingéd horse of poetry ought
to lie.   That is why we have no right to object
when the wingéd horse suddenly opens his
mouth and remarks in the words of Æsop:
"What a miserable cur!   He cannot eat corn

himself, nor will he allow others to eat it who can."

Had not the pragmatists issued a special claim upon reality, had they not, a little arrogantly, assumed the rights of leadership, no one would hold them responsible now for the general aimlessness of our life. Drift is their abhorrence too, and in many directions they have pointed out the road to mastery. Moreover, pragmatism was formulated by two thinkers who, in their feeling for reality, in their acceptance of a human nature that calls nothing common or unclean, and in their desire to make human nature more conscious of itself, might well be called rather poets than philosophers. They were poets, yes; but they were not *sufficiently* poets to intensify the conception of human nature that they had inherited from our tradition—their own vein of poetry, golden in Professor James, silver in Professor Dewey, ran too thin for that; and besides, their whole training had gone to make them students of the existing fact.   Unable as they were to alter the level of human vision, all they could do was to take men on the level where they found them and release their latent capacities on that level—an immensely valuable thing, of course, but not the vital thing for us, because it is the level itself that is at fault in America.   Had our existing fact, had the core of our life been rich, as it is, for example, in Russia, then their programme of liberation and control would have been as adequate for the nation in general as it now is for the few qualified individuals.   What it actually did was to unfold, for the most part, a human nature that was either detached from the sources of life or contented with a very primitive range of needs and desires.

That is why, though they are always cutting off the heads of the hydra that has us in its grasp, our pragmatic awakeners have really not only failed us but traduced us.   For our hydra is, and always has been, self-complacency, satisfaction with just the primitive scale of human values I speak of; and self-complacency, as a spiritual fact, is proof against all the arrows of the intelligence. Our awakeners accept themselves as a norm and by so doing become themselves a part of the very hydra that they attack. Assuming the intelligence as a final court of appeal, they are sealed against those impulses that give birth to self-criticism and the principle of growth; all they can do, therefore, is to unfold the existing fact in themselves, and in the world about them.

Does it matter that the founders of pragmatism, like certain of its English congeners, H. G. Wells, for example, have passed outside it in order to meet the critical issues of life? The mercurial pilgrim soul of Professor James had passed on to a strange polytheistic mysticism long before he died; H. G. Wells, under the stress of the war, has redoubled his quest of "God, the Invisible King"; and Professor Dewey has not denied the need of a national

faith in this country, to attain which we shall
certainly have not merely to do something other
than we normally do, but to be something other
than we normally are. Creators themselves,
and essentially poets, they have been free of
their own creations, they have shown that they
are members of the elect company of the "older
and bolder"; nevertheless, they have justified
a multitude of their followers in that complacent, mechanistic view of life to which
everything else in our mock-efficient, success-
loving society predisposes them. Enthroning,
as they have, the intelligence which merely sees,
in place of the imagination which sees and feels,
they have in their "practicality" sanctioned the
type of mind whose emotional needs are so limited that the efficient pursuit of some special
object is all that it demands of life.

II

Pragmatism has failed us, I say, because it
has attempted to fill the place that only a na-

tional poetry can adequately fill. Does any one imagine that we are the only people that has been reduced to the pulp-like, inelastic state in which we find ourselves to-day? Have we forgotten what Germany was like at the beginning of the nineteenth century, disjointed, vague and sentimental, for all the sporadic flames of her music and philosophy? And have we forgotten how Germany in a generation reached the wonderful maturity that preceded that plunge into imperialism which the bad old ways of the nineteenth century alone rendered inevitable? Our localists, our individualists, our American decentralizers may, if they choose, regard that process as an evil one, but if so they deny Goethe, the poet who, co-operating as it were with the Napoleonic wars, brought its dynamic unity to the German people. How did he do this? By projecting in *Faust* a personification of spiritual energy anchored by a long chain of specific incidents in the concrete experience of the German people and thereby infusing into that experience the leaven of development, impelling the individual to form himself into a peculiar being ever in search also of a conception of what men are collectively. By thus laying more and ever more demands upon human nature, by compelling men to accept that spirit of restless striving which gives them a leverage over things, he not only electrified the German people but obliged it to create an environment worthy of itself.

Now, it is of no importance at the moment that we have no Goethe in America and that we have no reason to suppose we are going to get one; it is of no importance that we cannot count on a messianic solution of our troubles, any more than we can count on the rude jolt which the war may, or may not, give us. What is important is for us to see that the really effective approach to life is the poetic approach, the approach that Goethe summed up in his phrase "from within outward," and that it is

the effective approach because it envisages
method in terms of value, every ounce of pres-
sure that is put upon value registering itself
with a tenfold intensity, so to speak, in the
sphere of application.

This has been the European approach from
time immemorial. Since the days of the ca-
thedral builders everything that we call the environment has come as a natural result of the
demands that human nature has laid upon itself.
Is this less true of the present day than of the
past? Has not the whole impetus toward social reform in modern England come about
through that intensification of the poetic view
of life which began with Carlyle's tremendous
restatement of the spiritual principle, which
passed over into the economic sphere with Ruskin and William Morris, and through which
English liberalism has since learned gradually
but effectively to assimilate science and use it as
a ship uses a search-light? Can any of our
awakeners take exception to the following pas-

sage in which Morris, actuated by his own lusty, creative joy in life and by his hatred, his vivid, compelling hatred of the ugliness of modern society, pointed out the path to reform from within outward?

"It was my good luck only that has put me on this side of the window among delightful books and lovely works of art, and not on the other side, in the empty street, the drink-steeped liquor shops, the foul and degraded lodgings. *I know by my own feelings and desires* what these men want, what could have saved them from this lowest depth of savagery: employment which would foster their self-respect, and win the praise and sympathy of their fellows, and dwellings which they would come to with pleasure, surroundings which would soothe and elevate them, reasonable labor, reasonable rest. There is only one thing that can give them this —Art."

Thus Morris, with his conception of "joy in labor," threw out in the midst of a machine

age a palpitant standard of living that will in
the end, especially now that it has come to light
again in the minds of English reconstruction-
ists, serve to delimit the essential function of
the machine in English society. And he did
this, precisely, by the "unrealistic" method of
projecting a Utopia, by seeing life in terms of
that imagination which knows how important
the intelligence is and is able to impel it in the
direction of a deeply desired goal. That Morris knew little of science and cared little for it
is beside the point; by laying demands upon
life, by insisting that human nature must be
creative, he obliged his contemporaries and his
successors to frame *through* science an environment that would make that consummation possible. That is why the English liberalism rep-
resented in various ways by Shaw and Wells
and Graham Wallas is so much more effective
than the liberalism of our awakeners, who,
while they have assimilated the ideas of all
these men, have been unable to share their im-

pulse. Shaw and Wells and Wallas, all of
whom are as much the heirs of Morris's peculiar socialism as they are of science, have ever
envisaged evolution in terms of a more stringent
demand upon life; not in terms of fine thinking merely but of "love and fine thinking," not
in terms of man merely but of self-surpassing
man, not in terms of efficiency merely but of
happiness, and all the other things have been
added unto them—the things which have made
possible, for instance, that beautiful programme
of the British Labor Party over which we were
all marveling the other day. Is it not a sufficient comment on our pragmatic awakeners that,
possessing no infectious ideal of "joy in labor,"
the best they can do is to publish unleavened
studies on the control of fatigue?

III

"I know by my own feelings and desires."
Why has no one been able to embrace our
American life in those dynamic personal terms

with which Morris embraced the life of England? Why has it been impossible for us to compass the poetic view of life that has proved itself in other countries capable of so many wonderful things? It is because we have never been able to make any complicated imaginative demand upon life. Our field of reality has required such an over-development of our acquisitive instincts that our creative instincts have had no scope at all; and consequently we have never been able to rise above those two equally uncreative conceptions of human nature, the total depravity of Puritanism and that optimistic self-complacency which is Puritanism's obverse and twin brother. Instead of a Carlyle we have had an Emerson, instead of a Morris we have had a Whitman—that is the whole story.

For Emerson's private perfectibility, based as it was on the idea that all we have to do to attain our majority is to look within ourselves and cast off the swaddling-clothes of tradition, led by an easy transition, our society being what

it was in the nineteenth century, into that conception of the "spontaneous man" which our
political democracy had inherited from Rousseau and which, splendidly amplified by Walt
Whitman, has weathered all the vicissitudes of
our thinking to the present day. "Time," said
Emerson, in words that might well be applied
to himself, "melts to shining ether the solid
angularity of facts"; is it remarkable that his
own subjective idealism went by default? Not
that one means to disparage Walt Whitman,
who has taught us all to accept life and rejoice
in it, but that Whitman's great work is to be
measured in terms not of general human experience but of a special situation: one has only
to recall that up to a generation ago our entire
race was conceived in the holy shame of a re-
luctant wedlock to realize the extent of our
national obligation to Whitman's robust animal
humors. But greater as Whitman was than
William Morris, he fulfilled a more primitive
need, a need that would never have existed had

it not been for our exclusively Puritan past; he was unable to carry us a step forward as Morris carried England, because, having embraced life, he was unable really to make anything of it. Where Morris, with his conception of "joy in labor," not only released the creative energies of men but held out before them a vision of excellence in labor that mobilized those energies and impelled men to reconstruct their environment in order to give them full play, Whitman merely universalized the miraculous animality that summed up his own experience. He knew nothing of what has been made of life, he was unable to imagine what can be made of life, over and above this miraculous animality. "Glad to be alive" simply, however intensely, he established a point of departure for the creative spirit—and there he left us. And there, so far as our poetical tradition is concerned, we have remained.

I resume all this because it explains why the pragmatists inherit no dynamic faith and why, lacking a dynamic faith, their treatment of society is itself so ineffective. It is in this lack of dynamic faith that they betray their unbroken descent from our old reformers and prove that pragmatism has not been the vital departure in our life that we have all been looking for. For what does it matter that our old reformers, ignorant of science, took for granted a "normal" human nature that was domestic and acquisitive, while our awakeners of the present day, equipped with a consummate scientific knowledge of mankind, take for granted a normal human nature that is efficient and sophisticated? At bottom they are all chips of the same block. Whittier, having risen to the heights of passion over the question of slavery, relapsed as soon as the war was over into a normal scale of values that enabled him to write that epic of satisfaction with things as they are, *Snow-Bound*. The muck-rakers of a later day having, at the rate of ten cents a word, abolished Peruna out of the world, passed on purified into the happy sphere in which Mr. Ray Stannard Baker now writes his *Adventures in Contentment*. And so it has been with the social workers and the big brothers of the settlement-house. Impelled to "give the other fellow a chance" to rise to the tepid status which life has portioned out to them and which they regard as highly fortunate and satisfactory, they have carried things to such a pass that immigrant sociologists, under the stimulus of a middle-class journalism, have been known to regard it as the highest dream of their hearts to be able to "lift" to the level of some ordinary American neighborhood into which they themselves have gained admittance men and women who are often immeasurably above it in the scale of the spirit.

This question of our immigrant population affords, I think, the most critical test of any merely pragmatic sociology. Our "hyphenates," bred in a richly poetic, a richly creative soil, desire to live poetically and creatively;

but they come to us as the detached limbs of a tree that they have left behind them. Has it never occurred to our awakeners that the only way in which we can absorb their life is by providing them with a new tree upon which they can engraft themselves and that the only hope of accomplishing this lies, not in improving their environment, in offering them comfort, in minimizing fatigue and shortening hours of labor, important as all these things are, by the way, but in quickening our own consciousness, in puncturing our own complacency, in rising by the force of our own demands upon life to that sphere of joyous activity where we ourselves are able to shed light and communicate warmth? This a pragmatic sociology cannot accomplish; nor can it be accomplished except through an appeal from sociology to the higher court of literature. Incapable of the poetic view of life and repudiating it, the pragmatists are able only to codify our society, to rearrange the allegiances that already exist, and to impose upon the American people programmes which have sprung from the poetic vision of other countries and which they have assimilated through their intelligence alone. Self-sufficient as they are, committed by the weakness of their imagination and by the analytical habitude of their minds to a mechanistic view of human nature, they are unable to fuse and unify our wills, they are unable to communicate any of those vital incentives which are the austere fruits not of "interest" but of love. Did I say that, possessing no infectious ideal of "joy in labor," the best they can do is to concentrate their minds on the control of fatigue? No, they can do one thing better; they can evade reality altogether and say with Mr. Henry Ford that "no man can take pride in his work *until* he gets something for it, *until* he has leisure to enjoy life." In this way, throwing up the sponge altogether, accepting machinery and more machinery and still more machinery as a *fait accompli*, and giving up all hope of determining

the rational place of machinery in life, they can
tell every one except the favored few whose
sophistication enables them to glut their intelligence on that strange freak the American soul,
to seek reality in anything else than their work
—riding about the country in Ford cars, on
Sundays, for example, with their mouths open.
Such is the destiny of the working class, as our
young pragmatic intellectuals see it.   As to the
middle class, they can in time, by consummat-
ing their freedom and capping it with control,
attain the more discreet paradise that the Pierce-
Arrow Company is at last able to place at their
disposal.

IV

So, becalmed as we are on a rolling sea, flap-
ping and fluttering, hesitating and veering
about, oppressed with a faint nausea, is it
strange that we have turned mutinous not only
against our old leaders, the colonial, fire-eating
minor prophets of Wall Street and their liter-

ary and philosophical standard-bearers, but also against our awakeners, the pragmatists, and the human nature that they wish to liberate in its own vicious circle, a human nature impoverished by hard, primitive conditions which has fulfilled the prophecy John Stuart Mill made with regard to industrialism in general, that it threatened the world with a "deficiency of preferences"?

Let us put it to our awakeners themselves. They say that we are born too late in a world too old to be able to compass anew the poetic view of life that has actuated the societies of Europe. They say that our blood is too mixed and our aims too diverse for us to achieve a national faith in the European sense. But what are they able to suggest as a substitute? We have no American culture, no; but we have an "American spirit," the spirit which has produced Sousa's music and Christy's art and Mrs. Eddy's religion. Are they satisfied with this? We have none of the unity that gives life, no;

but we have almost succumbed to the uniformity that destroys it. Are they pleased with this? Whether they subscribe to the "melting-pot" theory or believe in "preaching hyphenation," have they not proved themselves, in fact, bankrupt in solutions? They have, and it is because they have not entered into themselves, these awakeners of ours. "I know by my own feelings and desires," said Morris of the English workingmen of his time, "what these men want." When we have "feelings and desires," when, rather, we have poets to formulate them, to create for us emblems of a greater life, magnetic ideals grounded in our own field of reality, then our social problems, effectively handled by the very minds that fumble now because they cannot distinguish between ideals and methods, will begin to solve themselves.

Let no one imagine then that we have outgrown the poetic view of life; we have simply not grown up to it, we have not yet reached that full consciousness where faith and purpose, the hallmarks of the mature kind, are able to subjugate to their own ends the machinery of existence. "For life to be fruitful," said George Sand, "life must be felt as a blessing." But to love life, to perceive the miraculous beauty of life, and to seek for life, swiftly and effectively, a setting worthy of its beauty—this is the acme of civilization, to be attained, whether by individuals or by nations, only through a long and arduous process. But is it not true that human nature, at bottom the same the world over and at all times, irresistibly desires life and growth? And is it not true that human nature, in its infinite complexity, responds now with one set of faculties, now with another, according to circumstances and the quality of its leadership? If our poetic life is at present in the most rudimentary state and beset with fallacies of every kind, consider what our circumstances have been, and remember that

our leadership in the past has not only not en-
couraged it, but has over-stimulated those very
elements in our make-up that most retard its
development.

CHAPTER VI

TOWARD THE FUTURE

So I return to the beginning of my enquiry. An organized higher life: that is what the world demands of us, that is what we have at last come to demand of ourselves.

An organized higher life,—in other words, in the first place, a literature fully aware of the difficulties of the American situation and able, in some sense, to meet them. For poets and novelists and critics are the pathfinders of society; to them belongs the vision without which the people perish. Our literature in the past has failed to produce sufficient minds capable of taking that supreme initiative; in consequence, it has fallen by its own weight under the chaos of our life. But for this it has not only the best of excuses, it has also at least one extraordinary precedent. Could there be a stranger parallel to the state of our literature to-day than the state of German literature in 1795, as Goethe describes it in the following words?

"Germany is absolutely devoid of any central point of social culture, where authors might associate with one another and develop themselves by following, each in his own special branch, one aim, one common purpose. Born in places far remote from each other, educated in all manner of ways, dependent as a rule upon themselves alone and upon the impressions of widely different surroundings; carried away by a predilection in favor of this or that example of native or foreign literature, driven to all kinds of attempts, nay, even blunders in their endeavor to test their own powers without proper guidance; brought to the conviction, gradually and only after much reflection, that they ought to adopt a certain course, and taught by practice what they can actually do;

ever and anon confused and led astray by a
large public devoid of taste and ready to swal-
low the bad with the same relish with which
it has previously swallowed the good,—is there
any German writer of note who does not recognize himself in this picture, and who will not
acknowledge with modest regret the many times
that he has sighed for the opportunity of sub-
ordinating at an earlier stage of his career the
peculiarities of his original genius to a general
national culture, which, alas! was nowhere to
be found? For the development of the higher
classes by other moral influences and foreign
literature, despite the great advantage which
we have derived therefrom, has nevertheless
hindered the Germans, as Germans, from developing themselves at an earlier stage."

How keenly our conscientious writers of the
older generation must have experienced that regret, those, I mean, who have never quite sub-
mitted to the complacent colonialism that has
marked so much of our culture in the past!

But, unfortunately, they have left no testimonies behind them. They have considered it so much an obligation to justify American life merely as American life that they have glossed over their own tragedies, not realizing perhaps that in this way they have glossed over also the failure of those higher aims that they themselves were born to represent. "Not the fruit of experience, but experience itself, is the end." That is the essential European doctrine, and it is because Europeans value life as such that so great a part of their vital energy goes into the production of minds capable of heightening that value, minds that are able to keep the ball of life rolling in the sight and to the glory of all. But that, as I have tried to show, was not the doctrine of our forebears; quite the contrary, indeed. In consequence, the writers of the younger generation inherit all the difficulties of their elders, and at compound interest.

For the intellectual life is sustained by the emotional life; in order to react vigorously

against one's environment one must in some
degree have been emotionally nurtured by it.
Our gifted minds lack too generally a certain
sort of character without which talent is altogether fickle and fugitive; but what is this character if it is not the accumulated assurance, the
spiritual force that results from preceding generations of effort along the lines toward which
talent directs us? Professor Brückner points
out in his history of Russian literature that "the
direct transition from uncultured strata to
strenuous mental activity is wont to avenge itself: the individual succumbs sooner or later to
the unwonted burden." And as for us young
people, how often do we not wear ourselves
out constructing the preliminary platform without which it is impossible to create anything!
We have so few ideals given us that the facts
of our life do not instantly belie. Is it strange,
therefore, that we have, unlike the peoples of
Europe, no student class united in a common
discipline and forming a sort of natural breed-

ing ground for the leadership that we desire?

Nevertheless, a class like this we must have, and there are, I think, many signs that such a class is rapidly coming into existence. To begin with, the sudden contraction of the national cultures of Europe during the war, owing to which many currents of thought, formerly shared by all, have been withdrawn as it were from circulation, has thrown us unexpectedly back upon ourselves. How many drafts we have issued in the past upon European thought, unbalanced by any investment of our own! The younger generation have come to feel this obligation acutely. At the same time they have been taught to speak a certain language in common by the social movements of the last twenty years. Acquainted through study and travel with ranges of human possibility which their ancestors were able to contemplate only in the abstract, they feel that the time has come to explore these possibilities and to test them out on our own soil. They see that Americans have never so much as dreamed of a radically more beautiful civilization, our Utopias having been so generally of the nature of Edward Bellamy's, complex and ingenious mechanisms, liberating the soul into a vacuum of ennui.   They see that it is art and literature which give the soul its higher values and make life worthy of interces- sion, and that every effective social revolution has been led up to and inspired by visionary leaders who have shown men what they might become and what they miss in living as they do. "Thought," according to one of the greatest of modern philosophers, "is strong enough to dis- turb the sense of satisfaction with nature; it is too weak to construct a new world in opposition to it."   Only desire can do this, they feel, these Americans of the new age; that is what separates them not only from our traditional leaders, but also from our awakeners, the prag- matists, who are so busily unfolding the social order of which they form an integral part.

They feel this, I say; they feel it very deeply.

How deeply they desire another America, not like the America of to-day, *grande et riche, mais désordonnée*, as Turgeniev said of Russia, but harmonious and beneficent, a great America that knows how to use the finest of its gifts! And have they not seen, rising about them on the wings of a warm, humane, concerted endeavor, nation after nation, casting off whatever incubus of crabbed age, paralysis, tyranny, stupidity and sloth has lain most heavily upon the people's life, checking the free development of personality, retarding the circulation of generous ideas? The Young Italy of Mazzini's day, the Young Ireland of ours, the rebirth of the submerged nationalities of Eastern Europe, reborn not to the greater glory of imperialism but in the name of an incalculably rich international humanity that beckons from the future— have they witnessed again and again that sudden fusion of great natural aggregations of men by which all their elements have been set beating together at the highest pitch, without feeling, to the bottom of their hearts, that civilization ought to be a symphony and that there is in mankind an orchestral instinct that is even now clamoring at the gates of consciousness?

I do not say that there is in this fact any presentiment of unison for us. Too many of the best minds of our own younger generation have already, owing to the aridity of our cultural soil, fallen victims to the creeping paralysis of the mechanistic view of life. Too many, more poetically endowed, have lost themselves in a confused and feeble anarchism. Too few Americans are able even to imagine what it means to be employed by civilization.

But certainly no true social revolution will ever be possible in America till a race of artists, profound and sincere, have brought us face to face with our own experience and set working in that experience the leaven of the highest culture. For it is exalted desires that give their validity to revolutions, and exalted desires take form only in exalted souls. But has there ever been a time when masses of men have conceived these desires without leaders appearing to formulate them and press them home? We are lax now, too lax, because we do not realize the responsibility that lies upon us, each in the measure of his own gift. Is it imaginable, however, that as time goes on and side by side with other nations we come to see the inadequacy of our own, we shall fail to rise to the gravity of our situation and recreate, out of the sublime heritage of human ideals, a new synthesis adaptable to the unique conditions of our life?

When that occurs, we shall begin to grow, as a people; and having begun to grow we shall grow quickly. For we already possess elements that belong to every level of development, even the highest; we possess them all, but they are not grouped in a vital order, they have no cumulative significance. As soon as the foundations of our life have been reconstructed and made solid on the basis of an experience of which we

have been shown the potentialities, all these ex-
traneous, ill-regulated forces will rally about
their newly-found center; they will fit in, each
where it belongs, contributing to the essential
architecture of our life. Then, and only then,
shall we cease to be a blind, selfish, disorderly
people. We shall become a luminous people,
dwelling in the light and sharing our light.